This journal belongs to:

_____

Promises for Life for Women Journal
Copyright © 2006 by The Zondervan Corporation
ISBN-10: 0-310-81586-X
ISBN-13: 978-0-310-81586-0

Journal quotations are taken from the *New Women's Devotional Bible*,
© 2006 by Zondervan. Produced with the assistance of the Livingstone Corporation
(www.Livingstonecorp.com). Project staff include Don Jones and Rachel Hawkins.

Product Manager: Kim Zeilstra
Design Manager: Michael J. Williams
Production Manager: Bev Stout
Design: Amy E. Langeler
Cover Photo: Getty Images/Karen Beard

Printed in the United States
06 07 08 / 4 3 2 1

PROMISES
for LIFE

for *Women*

JOURNAL

from the new international version

God created us to convey the distinctive imprint of his divine nature to a world often blinded to his existence. Even our differences reflect the One who delighted in creating a world of dazzling diversity: Peculiar penguins and majestic eagles; towering redwoods and dwarf pines; blondes, brunettes and redheads . . . every person created with the individual imprint of the Creator's hand to bear his image. So the next time you pass by a mirror, pause a moment to gaze in wonder at the designer original whom God loves so dearly—you!

I praise you because I
    am fearfully and
    wonderfully made;
your works are
    wonderful,
    I know that full well.
My frame was not
hidden from you
    when I was made in
    the secret place.
When I was woven
    together in the
    depths of the earth,
your eyes saw my
    unformed body.

Psalm 139:14–16

What do you take pride in? What keeps you from glorifying God? Has your focus become self-absorbed? Have you become self-glorifying? The solution is simple: Whatever is keeping you from God, give it to him for his glory. Let your relationship with Jesus be the source of your significance. When you humble yourself before God, you'll be lifted up.

The name of the Lord is
a strong tower;
the righteous run to it
and are safe.
The wealth of the rich is
their fortified city;
they imagine it an
unscalable wall.
Before his downfall a
man's heart is proud,
but humility comes
before honor.

Proverbs 18:10–12

God's plans are well worth waiting for. You may be tempted to take matters into your own hands, thinking God is just a little bit late. But don't risk God's perfect intentions for you by relying on your own schemes. Waiting for God's perfect timing can save you years of heartbreak. Remember, God is faithful and always keeps his promises . . . even if you have to wait.

My soul faints with
   longing for your
   salvation,
but I have put my
   hope in your word.
My eyes fail, looking for
   your promise;
I say, "When will you
   comfort me?"

Psalm 119:81–82

We all struggle with the difficulties of letting go of the old in order to grasp the new. Take heart. God understands that letting go of the familiar is hard. Yet he has called us to move on to new life in Jesus Christ by letting go of our old worldly lives, our old habits, our old dreams—to boldly move forward without looking back. When you feel God's call to move, allow him to guide you. He will give you the grace to do whatever he has asked.

We may think that a God of love would never allow his children to feel any pain. But sometimes God breaks us to make us better. He may break our hearts so we will make room for him there. He may break our will so we can discover his will for us. He may break our physical strength so we discover that God's strength is made perfect in our weakness. Like Jacob, the best response to God's tough love is to cling to him and earnestly pray, "I will not let you go unless you bless me."

Is there any sin God won't forgive? Maybe you think he won't forgive abortion. Maybe you think he won't forgive adultery. Or abandonment. Or alcoholism. Or abuse. And those are just the "As." But God's forgiveness encompasses the whole alphabet—A to Z. Jesus Christ paid for that forgiveness long ago—with his life. Jesus, whom Joseph foreshadowed, speaks kindly to us, "Your sins are forgiven."

Some children are born into loving homes where they are loved and nurtured. Others are born into situations from which they need to be protected. You may see this and realize how unfair the world is. You want to do something to make things right but feel sidelined. You wait. You watch. You pray. You want to perform some act of practical compassion. The truth is, sometimes the best action is the sideline action: Wait, watch, and pray. God will guide you to action when the time is right.

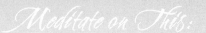

Meditate on This:

In the midst of our ordinary days—tending to our families, our jobs, our friends—how do we respond to the persistent pull of God's call? Regardless of how God makes his wishes known—a burning bush, a burning desire, or a burning need—are we willing to have our tidy plans and schedules interrupted to listen to his voice? Or are we too busy or too distracted to answer? Bottom line: Are we willing to be recruited at God's bidding?

God writes the law on our hearts so that we "will never walk in darkness, but will have the light of life." And he gives us that life so we can be a light in the world as well. As women we have unique opportunities to illuminate our families, our schools, our work-places—wherever we are called to live and work. Live the Ten Commandments; live connected to the light of the world. Shine, girl, shine. It seems our world has never needed it more.

The precepts of the
LORD are right,
giving joy to the
heart.
The commands of the
LORD are radiant,
giving light to the
eyes.

Psalm 19:8

People worship at the temple of self. They bow down to the god of money. They make sacrifices to elusive dreams of perfection—the perfect husband, the perfect family, the perfect body, the perfect life. Perfection becomes a substitute for the gold and jewels the Israelites used to create idols. As women, we often find it easier to worship temporal dreams of earthly perfection than the eternal God. The resplendent life we have planned shimmers before us, but the mirage will fail to satisfy our thirst.

Do you feel taken advantage of? Maybe it's time to engage some-one in conversation rather than detach from your relationship with them. Or maybe you've unintentionally mistreated a friend . . . you owe her money or lunch or a favor. Consider what needs to be done and take action: Repay the debt, replace the item, and apologize for a wrong. Do whatever it takes to restore the relationship. Do it because it pleases God and because your relationships will be richer for it.

Traffic's heavy. The freeway's jammed. The job's hard. My boss is unfair. The kids are screaming. No one loves me. My life is not as good as it ought to be! How long will this last? I want to go back! What do you long to return to? What is starting to look really good right about now? An old boyfriend? An old lifestyle? An old habit? Are you tempted to return? Rather than wandering in the desert, turn to the living water. He'll wash away the mountains of misery. He wants to fill you up, satisfy your hunger, and set you on the right track.

Applauding others can be surprisingly difficult. It's easy enough to fake it, to smile approvingly and nod in agreement. But sometimes when others are recognized for achievements, it's hard to feel anything but that ugly burning twinge of jealousy. Outwardly we're clapping and congratulating, but inwardly we slowly begin to simmer. Who does she think she is anyway? What's so special about her? Why all the fuss over one person? And if we don't catch it in time, that simmer can turn into a hard boil that erupts in anger, harsh words, and broken relationships.

God has made a place for you in his kingdom that only you can fill. You may be a Moses, out front leading the way. Or you may be serving in more behind-the-scenes ways like Miriam and Aaron. Your job is not to compare your work to another's and attach value based on what you can see. Your job is to turn down the heat of jealousy and quietly go about the work God has given you to do. When it's God's work, it's valuable. When we allow jealousy to . . . boil over, our own bitterness will only burn us.

Wandering through our day, thirsting for evidence of God's presence, hungry for the blessings everyone else seems to enjoy . . . stumbling blindly in the same old drudgery. We, too, can begin to doubt whether God is really guiding us, whether he really has chosen us. And if he has, why is life so hard? We mumble and grumble so loudly it's hard to hear God's voice. Stop. Look up to Jesus Christ. He took on your sin to heal your heart. He is the only way you can rid yourself of the venom of bitterness. Look up to him and live.

Do you sometimes think that God is limiting you rather than opening doors of opportunity because you are a woman? Then you believe the wrong press about him. God is the one who allowed women to inherit the land so long as they married into the same tribe. God is the one who put the Savior of the world into a woman's womb. He showed the risen Lord to women first, not men. God is not biased toward men; he's an equal-opportunity deity. When you give him your devotion, when you sit at his feet and learn from him, he'll treat you with dignity and give you the delights of your heart.

God provided a master guidebook for redesigning our spirits—the Bible. He directs us to tie his Word on our hands as we would tie a cord around a curtain; to bind his commandments to our foreheads as solidly as we would hang a valuable painting; to write his promises on our hearts as carefully as we would follow a blueprint. This is the ultimate form of home improvement.

Keep my words
  and store up my
    commands within you.
Keep my commands
  and you will live;
  guard my teachings
    as the apple of your
    eye.
Bind them on your
    fingers;
  write them on the
    tablet of your heart.
Say to wisdom, "You are
    my sister,"
  and call understanding
    your kinsman.

Proverbs 7:1–4

As believers, we're not really at war with "perfect" women. When you put yourself in their high-heeled sandals, you realize they have their own insecurities: Do people like me for me? Am I a slave to my looks? Opposition and uncertainties loom in every woman's heart. Do we really have to squeeze into the culture's mold to fit in? To get the man? To get the job? To have friends? So many times our internal struggles are the giants we must conquer. Conquering the heart and mind are the front line of the battle of faith.

It is God who arms me
with strength
and makes my way
perfect.
He makes my feet like
the feet of a deer;
he enables me to
stand on the
heights.
He trains my hands for
battle;
my arms can bend a
bow of bronze.
You give me your shield
of victory,
and your right hand
sustains me;
you stoop down to
make me great.

Psalm 18:32–35

A good mother wouldn't feed her children junk food or put her children in dangerous situations. She wants her children to grow strong and healthy, so they'll live long lives. So, too, a child of God learns to discipline her spirit, mind, and body, so as to become more Christ-like. To avoid what he forbids so that she can stay strong. To eat what is good for her body and take in that which feeds her mind and spirit.

I have seen you in the
    sanctuary
  and beheld your
    power and your
    glory.
Because your love is
    better than life,
  my lips will glorify
    you.
I will praise you as long
    as I live,
  and in your name I
    will lift up my
    hands.
My soul will be satisfied
    as with the richest
    of foods;
  with singing lips my
    mouth will praise
    you.
On my bed I remember you;
  I think of you through
    the watches of the
    night.
Because you are my
    help,
  I sing in the shadow
    of your wings.
My soul clings to you;
  your right hand
    upholds me.

Psalm 63:2–8

Meditate on This:

Think about the homeless man who approaches you for a handout on your way to work. I don't want to give him money, you justify, because he'd use it to buy alcohol or drugs. But what would Jesus do for him? He would be openhearted and openhanded, not hard-hearted and tightfisted. What could you do? Be resourceful! Carry some gift certificates or extra sandwiches when you pack your own lunch. Maybe you could clean out your closet and offer him a warm coat or blanket. Simply treating him like a human being might be the best portrayal of God's love.

From birthstones to gravestones, diamond rings to marble statues, humankind has used stones from time immemorial to mark significant life changes: births, deaths, engagements, victories in war, monuments to great people. What is it that makes stones such perfect material for the job? They're durable, slow-to-age, solid, and often very beautiful. Stones symbolize a permanence reaching beyond our short, human life spans.

He is the Rock, his
    works are perfect,
and all his ways are
    just.
A faithful God who does
    no wrong,
upright and just is he.

Deuteronomy 32:4

Have you been feeling that you are in a holding pattern, that your circumstances are not changing? Do you long to have resolution, to experience even a small victory? God is working even while you are waiting. Think of this time of waiting as a process that will eventually culminate in a victory. In the meantime, remain faithful and know that God is there with you, preparing you for the battles, goals, and victories to come.

God may or may not use a sign to speak to you. But he surely will give you what you need. In the midst of your doubts, ask for faith. When you face a challenge and fear making a mistake, ask him to give you wisdom and direction from his Word. When you feel unequal to some task and need encouragement, pray for the conviction, courage, and assurance of God's presence.

Our faith promises new life. God knows the "deaths" you've experienced. His plans for you are good, though they may look different than you expected. Rest in the knowledge that God uses every circumstance to strengthen your faith in him. When you think that life as you know it is over, remember the One who said, "I am making everything new" (Revelation 21:5).

Probably the hardest thing for me to surrender to God—and this may sound silly because you may be expecting me to say, "My children"—was the huge, five-bedroom home I purchased five years after my divorce. I knew that my home belonged to God and that I was simply a steward of what he had entrusted to me, but that didn't keep it from becoming an idol. My wonderful house in its expensive zip code supplied status. I couldn't imagine giving it up, especially if God wanted me to live somewhere I didn't like.

> I lie down and sleep;
>   I wake again because
>   the LORD sustains
>   me.
> I will not fear the tens
>   of thousands
> drawn up against me
>   on every side.
>
> **Psalm 3:5–6**

Be prepared when you're in a place of outward silence and sanctuary: as you lay awake in the early hours of the morning, while you wait in your car for your children to get out of school, when you walk the dog in the evening. Seek an inner silence and sanctuary also: Let go of mental noise and emotional confusion. Breathe deeply in and out until your heart and respiration rate slow. Humbly and receptively invite God to speak to you, and wait with faithful and obedient readiness.

My soul yearns, even
    faints,
  for the courts of the
    LORD?
my heart and my flesh
    cry out
  for the living God . . . .
Better is one day in
    your courts
  than a thousand
    elsewhere.

Psalm 84:2, 10

David and Jonathan's deep friendship was based not on family ties or warm, fuzzy feelings; they were bound by dedication to God and steadfast commitment to one another. Rather than being jealous of David for usurping his potential place as king, Jonathan accepted God's plan to make David king, sacrificially stepping down and supporting his friend.

A man of many
  companions may
  come to ruin,
but there is a friend
  who sticks closer
  than a brother.

Proverbs 18:24

The next time you feel misunderstood or mistreated, remember that you're following in some pretty big footsteps. King David was persecuted for doing God's bidding and did not retaliate when he was attacked. Jesus, the sinless God-man, was persecuted and died for our sins, yet he willingly forgave from the cross those who had tormented him. What will you do the next time you're wronged?

"If your enemy is
    hungry, feed him;
if he is thirsty, give
    him something to
    drink.
In doing this, you will
    heap burning coals
    on his head."
Do not be overcome by
    evil, but overcome
    evil with good.

Romans 12:20–21

Hannah Hurnard says an intercessor is "one who is in such vital contact with God and with his fellow men that he is like a live wire closing the gap between the saving power of God and the sinful men who have been cut off from that power."

Set a guard over my
mouth, O LORD?
keep watch over the
door of my lips.
Let not my heart be
drawn to what is evil,
to take part in wicked
deeds
with men who are
evildoers;
let me not eat of their
delicacies.

Psalm 141:3–4

Do we ever, like King David, celebrate God's blessings without concern for what others may think? Do we rejoice over the beauty of his creation or give him unrestrained praise for his loving-kindness and faithfulness? We don't have to shake tambourines to exhibit hearts of worship. Our rejoicing may be outwardly exuberant or quietly subdued. Our praise may be either public or private. But when our hearts are filled with gratitude, outward expressions of praise will naturally overflow.

But may all who seek you
    rejoice and be glad in you;
may those who love your
    salvation always say,
    "The LORD be exalted!"

Psalm 40:16

We all long for sanctuary. Crippled by sin, we enter God's presence with death hanging over our heads. But when we accept Jesus Christ's offer of eternal friendship, we receive eternal sanctuary at the King's table. At this feast, we will be given white robes to wear, and we will bow down in praise and adoration before the Prince of Peace.

Like a gathering cloud, worship encircles and protects God's people. It softens the soil of our hearts like nourishing rain. When we've been in a dark place and long for colorful beauty to replace the hardness that has settled into our scorched souls, simple acts of worship can prepare the way for God's words of wisdom to permeate our hearts. If your life seems parched, won't you allow God to paint a palette of colorful joy by spending time worshiping your Lord?

Rest assured that God is not offended when you come to him with your candid questions. He knows that wisdom is more valuable than any treasure on earth. You don't need to be the queen of a nation or travel to a distant land to seek the answers to your heart-felt questions; you simply need to open the pages of God's Word and go to him in prayer.

Choose my instruction
instead of silver,
knowledge rather than
choice gold,
for wisdom is more
precious than rubies,
and nothing you
desire can compare
with her.

Proverbs 8:10–11

Most of us have never been put in a position in which we had to choose between worshiping the true God or bowing down to statues made of wood or stone. Yet we often find ourselves tempted to try that balancing act while living in a spiritually and morally bankrupt culture. We may compromise our lifestyles, going to places or doing things we really know we shouldn't. We may even justify our behavior by saying we don't want to offend anyone.

We all need mentors like Elijah: women who have faced challenges and overcome; women who have grown through struggle and perseverance; women who have seen God perform miracles; women who have gone through hard times and experienced God's presence with them. These are the women who can pass on the news that God's Word is still active and dynamic among us. These are the ones who can place the mantle on our shoulders and confirm that we're ready to move on to greater tasks.

Is God asking you to take one step of obedience that may bring help and healing to another person? Perhaps it's as simple as taking up a pen and beginning a note of apology even though you're still hurting from what they did to you. Maybe you need to carve out time for the one thing you've been dreading to do. It could be you're compelled to take one act of firm discipline for the unruly child you love. That first step of obedience can bring your exception into a different light when you learn step by step what it means to trust God without exceptions.

> *If they obey and serve him,*
> *they will spend the rest of their days in prosperity*
> *and their years in contentment.*
>
> **Job 36:11**

The sad truth is that people do break promises. They fail to keep their word. And this breaks our hearts. But no matter how many promises have been broken, no matter how many people have let us down, God never will. He is faithful . . . even if his promises take time to come to fruition.

2 Corinthians 1:20
For no matter how many promises God has made, they are "Yes" in Christ. And so through him the "Amen" is spoken by us to the glory of God.

What do you do when you encounter a terrible scenario that seems to have no solution? When tragedy roars down on you like a tsunami? When something or someone truly terrifying marches your way? Do you curl up in retreat? Do you strike back in retaliation? Or do you lay the situation out before God and trust him to show you what to do? Wouldn't it be wonderful if down the road everyone who looks at the end of your story has reason to exclaim, "Who is a God like yours?"

How our lives are summarized depends on the choices we make each day. We have the tendency to become distracted with the cares and responsibilities of life. Laundry piles up. Bills need to be paid. Children get sick. As we care for our families and do our work, it's easy to become sidetracked from our primary purpose: pleasing God. It is easier to give lip service to spiritual things than to stay on course, keeping in step with the Spirit.

If we develop eyes to see, God will give us glimpses of himself through the beauty of nature: a blooming rosebush, a glorious sunset, a soft snowfall. Take time to whisper a prayer of adoration. You can also place reminders around your home or office to trigger thoughts of God: your favorite Bible sitting by the chair; books, music, and artwork placed in prominent positions. Don't let a day go by after which you wonder, Did I think about God today?

Times of thanksgiving need not be reserved for momentous occasions. Consider the countless reasons you have to be grateful. Has something brought great joy to your life? If not today, how about yesterday, or last week or last month? Consider the attributes of those you love: your husband's faithfulness, your friends' trustworthiness, your parents' goodness, your child's tender heart.

Shout for joy to the
    LORD, all the earth.
Worship the Lord with
    gladness;
come before him with
    joyful songs.
Know that the LORD is
    God.
It is he who made us,
    and we are his;
we are his people, the
    sheep of his pasture.
Enter his gates with
    thanksgiving
and his courts with
    praise;
give thanks to him
    and praise his name.
For the Lord is good
    and his love
    endures forever;
his faithfulness
    continues through
    all generations.

Psalm 100:1–5

We can't always finish what we start. That idea often runs counter to our sensibilities as women. Of course we have to finish. We have daily planners. We have to-do lists. We have people depending on us. We hate loose ends. We have every intention of completing what we begin. But sometimes we're supposed to leave some loose ends dangling. The simple truth is that loose ends leave room for someone else to come along and continue the work in new and unique ways. God may want you to move forward to a different phase of life.

Joshua 11:15
As the LORD commanded his servant Moses, so Moses commanded Joshua, and Joshua did it; he left nothing undone of all that the LORD commanded Moses.

God knows the agony of loving those who, at present, want nothing to do with him. Think of all the people he created who openly reject him. Yet he still loves them and shows by example that his "kindness leads [them] toward repentance" (Romans 2:4). In your own circumstances, follow God's example by being kind, but firm. Be faithful to keep yourself wholly holy. By doing this you can help bring your husband, parent, child, colleague, or friend to true belief.

You may not see yourself as a woman of influence. You may even shy away from sharing your faith with your kids, friends, family, or coworkers. But there are many ways you can make a difference. You can refuse to give in to peer pressure or to give up on a prodigal. You can speak out in the voting booth or on the editorial page. When you stand up for God's standards, you might be surprised— like a small pebble thrown into a large body of water, your words, actions, and prayers can ripple outward if you muster up the courage to take a stand.

Most likely you will not be chosen to rule a country, but you are the queen of your castle—your home. So what is the first thing on your to-do list each day? What is your number one priority? Eliminate your kids' hunger? Disarm family disputes? Tackle the budget? Or, when you get up, do you put your house in order by first putting your heart in order? The best way to run a home, a business, or a country is from your knees in prayer.

Give ear to my words,
  O LORD,
    consider my sighing.
Listen to my cry for
  help,
    my King and my God,
    for to you I pray.
In the morning, O LORD,
    you hear my voice;
  in the morning I lay
    my requests before
    you
  and wait in expectation.

Psalm 5:1–3

God wants us to know his joy now. Not tomorrow, not when we're healed, not when sorrow has passed, not when we've become successful, not when our child or spouse changes, not when we've lost ten pounds, not when we've paid off our debt, received a promotion or bought a bigger home, but now—on this day! Lasting joy does not reside in God's blessings, God's favor, God's gifts or God's people, but in God himself. Take time this day to seek the Lord and draw upon him to find your joy—your strength.

Create in me a pure
heart, O God,
and renew a steadfast
spirit within me.
Do not cast me from
your presence
or take your Holy
Spirit from me.
Restore to me the joy of
your salvation
and grant me a
willing spirit, to
sustain me.

Psalm 51:10–12

Meditate on This:

Many of us may think we're safe from the type of persecution Rosa Parks and Esther faced. But Christians are being persecuted throughout the world in places like China, the Sudan, and North Korea. Every day people die for the privilege of worshiping Jesus. Some people do not really know or understand the person and mission of Jesus and will take every opportunity to slander his followers. Wherever God has placed you, he can use you to speak his truth—words of love, justice, and faith to a lost world—even if it means being misunderstood or ridiculed.

As mere mortals, it's simply not possible to look beyond heaven's veil to see why God allows things to happen as they do. The simple truth is that God is God, and we are not. And let's face it: Sometimes the things that happen don't seem fair. But thankfully, God has sent an arbitrator in the form of his Son, Jesus Christ, to mediate between humans and holy God.

Meditate on This:

Are there circumstances that you cannot understand? Instead of trying to fix them or control them, rather than trying to figure out the what, when, where, and why of your struggles, focus instead on Whom: God is Elohim—the Creator, who made you for a purpose. God is El Elyon—God Most High, whose ways are higher than our ways. God is El Roi—the God who sees and knows where you are and how you feel. God is El Shaddai—the Lord God Almighty, the one who can change you or walk you through your circumstances as surely as he can send rain from heaven.

Do you not know?
  Have you not heard?
The LORD is the ever
  lasting God,
  the Creator of the
  ends of the earth.
He will not grow tired or
  weary,
  and his understanding
  no one can fathom.
He gives strength to the
  weary
  and increases the
  power of the weak.

Isaiah 40:28–29

Meditate on This:

The book of Psalms is a wonderful place to introduce yourself to the idea of delighting in God's Word. The poetic music of the psalms is rich in metaphors and images that let your imagination soar with the grandeur, majesty, wisdom, and unsurpassing love of God. You will see him as a rock, a fortress, a strong tower, a nurturing mother, and so much more. He rides on the wind and shows himself in the starry heavens. Delight yourself in singing along with the psalmist and plant your roots deep in the nourishing living water of God's Word.

Blessed is the man
    who trusts in the
    LORD,
    whose confidence is
    in him.
He will be like a tree
    planted by the water
    that sends out its
    roots by the stream.
It does not fear when
    heat comes;
    its leaves are always
    green.
It has no worries in a
    year of drought
    and never fails to
    bear fruit.

Jeremiah 17:7–8

The natural world is a testimony to God's magnificent creatorship and is also the object of our diligent stewardship. We must flee the two extremes—either fearing nature's power or worshiping creation and not the Creator. Even today, the creation is God's universal proclamation of his nature, underpinning his special revelation through Christ and the Scriptures. As women who love and appreciate the beauty of the world, may we always remember to listen closely to the deeper truths of God's goodness and grandeur that whisper from the rushing stream or shout from the thunderclap.

Romans 8:18–21

I consider that our present sufferings are not worth comparing with the glory that will be revealed in us. The creation waits in eager expectation for the sons of God to be revealed. For the creation was subjected to frustration, not by its own choice, but by the will of the one who subjected it, in hope that the creation itself will be liberated from its bondage to decay and brought into the glorious freedom of the children of God.

If you long for greater intimacy with God, ask him to examine your heart to see if there are any areas in which you need to come clean before him. Confession, in its most elemental form, simply means agreeing with God that you've departed from his ways and fallen short of his standards. Admit to him—and to yourself—that you are in need of a spiritual bath.

Hide your face from my sins
and blot out all my iniquity.
Create in me a pure heart, O God,
and renew a steadfast spirit within me.

Psalm 51:9–10

Sometimes we change the name to cover our sin: It's not gossip, it's sharing; It's not coveting, it's admiring; It's not lying, it's explaining. David even planned to have his lover's husband killed in war to make the object of his lust a widow, thinking that would redefine adultery. But God didn't buy it. O God, have mercy. God doesn't forgive excuses. But God does forgive sin. He's waiting for us to call it what he calls it—sin.

Cleanse me with hyssop,
and I will be clean;
wash me, and I will
be whiter than
snow.
Let me hear joy and
gladness;
let the bones you
have crushed
rejoice.
Hide your face from my
sins
and blot out all my
iniquity.

Psalm 51:7–9

When we feel weak-kneed and lack confidence, we are most open to relying on God. So if you find yourself in a new situation today, make sure you don't rely on your own limited talents or skills, but that you place your unshakable confidence in the limitless God. Nothing silences the voice of timidity as powerfully as the voice of Scripture.

Philippians 4:13
I can do everything through him who gives me strength.

Sometimes without realizing it, we project upon God images of our own making—a demanding taskmaster for whom we never can do enough, an exacting parent we can never quite please, a short-tempered boss we easily anger. Yet, this is not the God of the Bible, the God of David, and this is not the real God.

For as high as the
heavens are above
the earth,
so great is his love for
those who fear him;
as far as the east is
from the west,
so far has he removed
our transgressions
from us.
As a father has compas-
sion on his children,
so the LORD has
compassion on
those who fear him.

Psalm 103:11–13

Every morning around daybreak neighborhoods fill with bird-song. Referred to by bird-watchers as "the dawn chorus," the daily songfest marks a bird's territory and communicates to our ears a sound of reckless, warbling joy. True, birdsong is glorious, but only human beings sing words of praise. And our God who filled his universe with all sorts of wonderful extras wants our praise. He wants our praise. Why? Because God is worthy.

I will praise you as long
as I live,
and in your name I
will lift up my
hands.
My soul will be satisfied
as with the richest
of foods;
with singing lips my
mouth will praise
you.

Psalm 63:4–5

Our culture is not kind to aging women. Physical beauty and glamorized sexuality are prized above character and inner loveliness. God's view—the biblical view—of growing older makes the world's view of beauty seem silly and nonsensical. But it takes mental discipline to focus on God's standards of worth and beauty when so many media outlets suggest that anyone over thirty is past their prime.

> "Many women do
>   noble things,
> but you surpass
>   them all."
> Charm is deceptive,
>   and beauty is fleeting;
>   but a woman who
>   fears the LORD is to
>   be praised.
> Give her the reward she
>   has earned,
>   and let her works
>   bring her praise at
>   the city gate.
>
> **Proverbs 31:29–31**

How long has it been since you listed the good things God has given you? He created a beautiful world full of all you need: air, water, limitless choices of food, and much more. In giving you your family, your ability to smell, and your sense of humor, God has given you precious gifts. From telling Old Testament tales of his long-suffering to letting you see behind the scenes of his Son's trip to Earth, his Word is an extra special love gift.

God's wisdom isn't reserved for a few scholars; it's available to everyone. Wisdom is found in the book that holds eternal truth—God's Word. According to Solomon, wisdom comes from listening to God (one of the most frequent commands in the Old Testament) and obeying him. Wisdom comes from letting the Holy Spirit live within you.

> ### Galatians 6:7–10
> A man reaps what he sows. The one who sows to please his sinful nature, from that nature will reap destruction; the one who sows to please the Spirit, from the Spirit will reap eternal life. Let us not become weary in doing good, for at the proper time we will reap a harvest if we do not give up. Therefore, as we have opportunity, let us do good to all people, especially to those who belong to the family of believers.

Everybody hates something. And strange as it may seem, the Bible says that even the all-loving God hates some things. What are the top seven things you hate? To love God is to hate what he hates. Instead of despising cauliflower or hating slippery, icy roads, go a little deeper. Really think about what's on God's "hate" list. Then banish those things from your house and your heart.

> Let those who love the
> LORD hate evil,
> for he guards the lives
> of his faithful ones
> and delivers them
> from the hand of
> the wicked.
>
> **Psalm 97:10**

Perhaps you remember when someone's language wounded your spirit. Maybe you were torpedoed by a thoughtless comment from a neighbor or struck down by a destructive argument with a family member or friend. We have all experienced the withering force of cruel words. But consider the effects of good and kind speech. Just as foolish talk can bring death, truth spoken with love can lift the discouraged soul, restore dignity to the oppressed, and heal the brokenhearted.

Colossians 4:6
Let your conversation be always full of grace, seasoned with salt, so that you may know how to answer everyone.

There's only one metamorphosis that matters—and it will keep every woman eternally beautiful. It's a metamorphosis of the heart. Having a heart of unselfish service that has been transformed by Christ—that is what's important. And that is what gives us the ability to laugh at the future . . . even if it involves flabby thighs.

2 Corinthians 5:16–17
So from now on we regard no one from a worldly point of view. Though we once regarded Christ in this way, we do so no longer. Therefore, if anyone is in Christ, he is a new creation; the old has gone, the new has come!

You may have dreamed an impossible dream only to have it turn into a nightmare. Perhaps it was the dream of a perfect child who has turned into a challenging teenager. Maybe you dreamed of a new start but are now struggling to make a blended family work. Do what Joseph did when facing the impossible. Bring Jesus into your home and invite him into your heart. He can't comprehend the word impossible because with him all things are possible.

There's no such thing as a Christian who's been spoiled rotten with spiritual gifts. God gives us gifts that fit us perfectly, gifts that fill and complete us. How are we to respond to such generosity? By using those gifts to the utmost. Isn't that what every parent wants their child to do? We offer our children good things, so they'll know they are loved. But we want them to use their gifts often and take care of them.

James 1:17–18

Every good and perfect gift is from above, coming down from the Father of the heavenly lights, who does not change like shifting shadows. He chose to give us birth through the word of truth, that we might be a kind of firstfruits of all he created.

What kind of rest can Jesus offer when we spend so much time being busy, when we wear ourselves out trying to please everyone around us? Maybe that's the point. Maybe it's all the trying that makes us weary. But Jesus doesn't tell us to try, try, and try some more. He simply beckons us to come and learn from him. What a relief! We can lay down our effort and start learning to rest. We can rest in God's grace.

Philippians 4:4–7

Rejoice in the Lord always. I will say it again: Rejoice! Let your gentleness be evident to all. The Lord is near. Do not be anxious about anything, but in everything, by prayer and petition, with thanksgiving, present your requests to God. And the peace of God, which transcends all understanding, will guard your hearts and your minds in Christ Jesus.

Are you digging for buried treasure? If not, you should know that it's waiting there for you. For this kind of digging, you need other kinds of tools: your Bible, a concordance, and maybe a reliable commentary or two. And bring along your mind, heart, time, and a bit of patience. You'll find a wealth of God's wisdom that can only be found when you search for it as if you were digging for gold or silver buried beneath the earth's surface.

O my people, hear my
   teaching;
   listen to the words of
   my mouth.
I will open my mouth in
   parables,
   I will utter hidden
   things, things from
   of old—
what we have heard and
   known,
   what our fathers have
   told us.
We will not hide them
   from their children;
   we will tell the next
   generation
the praiseworthy deeds
   of the LORD,
   his power, and the
   wonders he has done.

Psalm 78:1–4

When Jesus calls us to follow him, he is looking for people who are willing to let go of the ordinary and look for the extraordinary. Sometimes that means we're called to leave everything—our nets and our families—and go where he tells us. Other times, following him means we keep doing what we've been doing, only with a shift in our perspective: We still change diapers, but we focus on raising godly children; We still do laundry, but as we do, we remember that we serve the God of holiness.

Brothers, think of what you were when you were called. Not many of you were wise by human standards; not many were influential; not many were of noble birth. But God chose the foolish things of the world to shame the wise; God chose the weak things of the world to shame the strong. He chose the lowly things of this world and the despised things—and the things that are not—to nullify the things that are, so that no one may boast before him. It is because of him that you are in Christ Jesus, who has become for us wisdom from God—that is, our righteousness, holiness and redemption.

Many of us have probably secretly wondered if there is something wrong with us, if perhaps we just aren't trying hard enough to be good, conforming Christian women. So let's come together and identify ourselves to each other and the world. Let's discover and celebrate the fact that God has placed in the heart of many of his human creations an undercurrent so strong and so solid it carries us from birth to death.

I am still confident of
this:
I will see the goodness
of the LORD
in the land of the living.
Wait for the LORD
be strong and take
heart
and wait for the LORD.

Psalm 27:13–14

Throughout Scripture, God continually encourages us to rely on him like a child relies on a parent. Some of us may have lost the ability to trust because our parents never provided adequately for our needs, while others of us may have lost our ability to trust through circumstances—a failed job, the death of a loved one, a lost desire. But God has revealed time and again that he can help us relearn that childlike faith if we let him. It's a matter of cultivating a relationship with him and letting him show his faithfulness as he uncovers good from our circumstances.

We live in a youth-oriented culture. American women spend millions of dollars each year on products designed to keep them looking and feeling young. Older women can easily feel marginalized—as if their days of usefulness are past. Yet Scripture reminds us that God reserves some of his most significant assignments for women who have attained the maturity to handle them—like Anna the prophetess. When you set your heart to serve God, you can continue to do so whatever your health, age, or personal circumstances.

In the last days, God says,
I will pour out my
 Spirit on all people.
Your sons and daughters
 will prophesy,
 your young men will
 see visions,
 your old men will
 dream dreams.
Even on my servants,
 both men and
 women,
I will pour out my
 Spirit in those days,
and they will prophesy.

Acts 2:17–18

Some women have a gift for serving others, no matter what. They serve until they can't stand up anymore. And as soon as they're finished recuperating, they're up and at it again. You might be one of those women. You think, I don't have time to rest, and I really don't have time to be sick. But let's face it: Sometimes our human bodies have to throw in the towel and surrender. We get sick . . . or just sick and tired. That's when we can ask for help from the One who is the source of healing and strength.

Jesus, the master builder of strong, resilient women, likens our spiritual foundation to a building with a strong, immobile base. We know that sooner or later, floods will come in one form or another: illness, financial problems, a relationship breakdown, societal calamities, terrorism or natural disasters. If we don't take Jesus' words to heart and put them into practice, we are on shaky ground. But if we build our spiritual lives on what he says, we can withstand anything that shakes us.

Jesus spent three years searching . . . his entire ministry. Jesus still searches for the lost. Where did he find you? At a nightclub? Living life as a rebel? Riding the subway in a big city? Buried under a pile of books at a university? Or perhaps he found you sitting in a church pew, convinced you had everything together, that you could set things right with God on your own terms? Wherever you were, the Savior came looking for you because you are valuable to him. You were worth every moment of his search. For when you answered his call, he and the angels in heaven rejoiced.

Luke 19:10
For the Son of Man came to seek and to save what was lost.

It has been proven that physical changes occur when we fall in love: skin glows, eyes sparkle, heart rate increases. And for some of us, similar changes take place when we're expecting a child. Conventional wisdom says that "all brides are beautiful" and "pregnant women glow." It's chemical, hormonal, and very real. Why not at the spiritual level too? When you allow the Lord to fill your heart with his boundless love, it shows on the outside.

For the LORD takes
    delight in his people;
he crowns the humble
    with salvation.
Let the saints rejoice in
    this honor
and sing for joy on
    their beds.

Psalm 149:4–5

God promises that when we search for him, we'll find him and be satisfied. Imagine the God of the universe wanting you to reach out to him—waiting in eager anticipation. Do you know what's really remarkable? As you begin reaching toward God, you'll find you don't need to reach at all. He is not far. Our loving God is as close as your next breath—your next prayer.

We all have experienced suffering. What is your unique story? You may have suffered from a disease or a broken marriage. No matter how universal the trauma, your situation and your response are personal to you. Others can learn from what you have gone through. Ask God for opportunities to share what you've learned about God's grace through your experience with suffering.

Securing happiness on our own is like trying to catch the wind. We can try to chase it, but it will always remain just out of reach. The Bible teaches us that instead of searching for happiness, we should allow God's joy and peace to reign in our hearts. Instead of striving for the things we think will satisfy, we can learn to find true contentment by looking to God, whatever our circumstance. Don't waste your time trying to catch the wind; instead, find true happiness by laying hold of the Wind Maker.

> **Ecclesiastes 2:26**
> To the man who pleases him, God gives wisdom, knowledge and happiness, but to the sinner he gives the task of gathering and storing up wealth to hand it over to the one who pleases God. This too is meaningless, a chasing after the wind.

It's easy to think the past was better than today. Most of us have selective memories. We only remember what we want to remember. You can make the case that it's good to forget the bad. However, when we look at the past through rose-colored glasses, we run the risk of being ungrateful for what we have right now. Rather than seeing today's gifts, we yearn for yesterday's fun and games, conveniently glossing over the difficulties of the past.